CONTENTS

	Introduction	1
1	The purpose of an economic system	3
2	Wealth is good – regardless of how it is distributed	12
3	The simple logic of how wealth is created	18
4	Why wealthy people are beneficial to everybody	25
5	See Jack create new wealth	30
6	Value added through real estate appreciation	35
7	Enforcing socialism	37
8	Socialism in the modern world	42
9	The inclusiveness of capitalism	46

INTRODUCTION

The near total vacuum of basic economics knowledge by most people was a key reason for this book. The public education system in the United States is woefully inadequate when it comes to educating young people on the subject of economics in particular. Related to that is the dramatic positive shift in perceptions about socialism by young people today. This is due to a focus on social engineering by our public schools and universities in lieu of teaching actual economics. For that reason and others, a closer look at the differences between socialism and capitalism is warranted.

Another key reason for the book was to reveal how wealth is created in a society. The author discovered the exact mechanism of wealth creation after applying the Conservation Equations from engineering, to the rapidly increasing levels of wealth in the United States in past centuries. Understanding this simple mechanism of wealth creation leads to a new and profound respect for the value of businesses and entrepreneurs in a society. It also makes it clear what should and shouldn't be done to foster the ability of businesses to create wealth for the whole society, including the poor. How all this ties in with the differences between socialism and capitalism is examined in the following pages.

This book is both brief and easy to understand because it is focused on fundamental concepts. There are almost no statistics, details, graphs, numbers, equations, etc. here. While it is definitely readable in an hour, many people will get more out of it if they take their time, and reread different chapters later. The basic concepts are generally self-evident based on simple logic, even for those who have absolutely zero education or understanding of economics. If you understand what is presented here, and you should - as long as you can read and think, you will have a better understanding of key economic concepts than many of the "experts" who appear on television. Most of the so called "experts" in the media perceive "proper" economic systems from the standpoint of a desired economic outcome for everybody. You as the reader will perceive them based solely on reality. (Reality is better.) Key concepts are covered redundantly to aid learning.

There is no chapter on the concept of supply and demand, which is a cornerstone of economics. Instead, it is demonstrated with examples throughout the book. The value in this little book is in the easily understood and occasionally profound nature of the content, not the number of pages. You will have to think about what you're reading, but that's all. You will become a more intelligent member of society and a more informed voter as a result of learning the content that follows.

CHAPTER 1

THE PURPOSE OF AN ECONOMIC SYSTEM

The purpose of an economic system is to allocate the wealth that is generated by a society. It determines who gets how much. Why do some people make a lot more or less money than others? Is that good or bad? The answers to those questions are subjective and often depend on one's perception of the particular economic system involved. To explain that, let's first understand that there are two basic types of economic systems today. The United States and most other countries operate under a predominantly capitalistic economic system, often referred to as a "free market" economy or system. That description refers to the fact that almost all decisions about buying and selling goods and services, including employment compensation, are made by citizens who have free choices in such matters. Prices and production are determined by what people are willing to pay.

In contrast, Russia, Communist China, Cuba, Venezuela and a handful of other countries, operate under a predominantly socialistic economic system, sometimes called a "command economy". Prices and production are determined by what the government commands.

Under capitalism, fairness is generally based on a person's results in the workplace. It is considered fair under capitalism for a person who works hard enough to produce twice as much, to receive more compensation. Under socialism, fairness is based on being present. Everybody who shows up for work gets paid the same. Although it is certainly encouraged, productivity is not a consideration regarding pay, because socialism mistakenly assumes that everybody will work equally hard relative to their abilities. In theory, it protects those with limited abilities so that they earn the same as everyone else if they work just as hard. In reality, the main beneficiaries of the protection are those with limited motivation to contribute. Ironically, it is because of socialism that those who were once motivated and productive workers are the ones who become the demotivated, and usually then comprise the largest segment of the labor force. Much of the workforce develops a sense of futility from the realization that no amount of hard work will ever result in a better quality of life for the worker.

Socialistic economic systems generally require authoritarian or totalitarian governments to enforce adherence to them. Whether it's a high income, or personal wealth, people who are successful don't normally give up what they have worked for without coercion. Fascism is one type of authoritarian government. Nazism was form of fascism, specific to Hitler's Nazi party. Another type of authoritarian government is communism. Both fascism and communism force people to conform in their words and deeds to the state.

In a free market economy, prices and supplies of goods and services are self-adjusting based on everybody's decisions. In the socialistic, or command economy, production and prices are controlled by a central government authority. It is usually the ruling party bureaucrats. In theory, the assets of the people such as businesses and infrastructure are owned collectively by the people, but in practice, the members of the ruling government that controls everything are effectively the owners.

As a point of interest, Karl Marx, a German who lived in the 1800's is the namesake of the term Marxism. He and Friedrich Engels wrote *The Communist Manifesto*, and he is commonly considered the "Father of Socialism." Socialism is a broad philosophy that also pertains to eliminating differences between the various classes in a society through such means as the "collective" (government) ownership of businesses and other institutions.

US schools often teach that Scandinavian countries like Sweden and Norway have successfully introduced a "democratic socialism." They teach that true socialism can coexist naturally with democracy. In the real world, these countries have democratic governments with some specific systems such as health care that they operate in a generally socialistic manner. Democratic governments can impose policies that have socialistic properties, without becoming authoritarian or forcing socialism on the overall economy. As is the case everywhere, businesses and workers in these Scandinavian countries do best when they are least encumbered by socialistic policies.

Both capitalistic and socialistic economic systems are in place for the purpose of distributing the wealth generated by the workforce of a country, to the workers. Each does it very differently than the other. In a capitalistic economy, wealth is generally distributed at proportionately greater levels to those individuals who proportionately contribute more to the success of the economy. When you view it on a closer level, wealth distribution is more clearly differentiated based on the level of contribution by different workers to the success of a company. The CEO makes more than the mail room clerk. The top producing sales rep typically makes more than the under producing sales rep. The nature of the economic system of capitalism is to incentivize companies not just to survive, but to compete and adapt and grow. That is done by incentivizing employees to produce results that are superior to the results of their competitors. Therein lies a universal cause and effect relationship. People work harder (effect) when you give them a tangible/financial reward (cause) for putting in the extra time and effort to produce better results. With sufficient incentive, employees will eagerly respond by becoming much more productive.

In the environment of capitalism, "superior" performance is judged on results. It is not based on superior effort. The employee that can perform at a high level with modest effort is more valuable to a company than the employee who expends tremendous effort, but for whatever reason produces marginal results. Results are all that really matter to a company at the end of the business cycle. Ultimately it is results that determine the success or failure of a company. Companies therefore pay keen attention to how their different employees perform in their positions, and look for ways to get the best results from each employee and each position. Larger companies often have the luxury of moving underperforming employees into positions that better fit their abilities, or sending them for skills training. But if an employee is unsuited for a particular job, it is in everyone's best long term interest for that employee to be replaced by someone more capable. Many very successful people failed at early jobs before they found their niche.

A simple example for wealth allocation as a function of performance is a professional sports team. The superstar athlete that contributes disproportionately to the success of his team will become a target for acquisition by other teams as soon as his contract is up. Smart managers in sports and other businesses will pay their top producers very competitively to acquire and keep them. Within individual companies, the more productive worker is the one more likely to be rewarded with a promotion and pay raise. The same process applies to companies themselves. More productive companies outperform their competitors, and they grow their income as they are rewarded for superior performance by the marketplace. If they are publicly traded companies, their stock values tend to increase. Less productive companies may find themselves filing for bankruptcy protection or just closing their doors. Capitalism financially incentivizes both employees and companies to perform better. The connection between employees and companies is important to understand. Companies are really just "teams" of employees. Here again, the sports analogy is valid. When the players on a team play at a higher level than their opponents, their team usually wins. The same holds true when the employees of a company perform at a higher level than their counterparts at a competing company. In the competition of a free market economy, companies push each other to do better. This results in a market with better products and lower prices over time.

The premise of socialism is: "From each according to his ability, to each according to his needs" (Karl Marx - 1875). It means everyone does as much as they are able, and gets enough to meet their needs. People don't need big houses or luxuries. They just need enough to live and maybe raise a family. So everybody has pretty much the same needs, and therefore receives about the same compensation. The economy's wealth is distributed as pay to the workers evenly, regardless of each individual's actual contribution toward the achievement of the organization's goals. In communist countries which control everything, socialism spans virtually all business organizations across the country, and everyone in the workforce makes about the same under the assumption that everyone works equally hard. As it turns out, that assumption is seldom even close to reality.

In contrast, capitalistic economies are governed by the laws of "supply and demand." Things cost more when they are harder to get, meaning the demand is higher. That is usually due to a reduced supply of those things, either because more people want them and the store shelves have been depleted, or because there are fewer of them available for reasons of low production. Regardless of the reason, the demand is high relative to the supply, and the prices self-adjust upwards when people are willing to pay more. Companies then have a profit motive to chase those higher selling prices by making more of the products, which increases the supply. The shortage of those products then goes away, and the prices stabilize or come back down because there is then less demand for them. People no longer want them badly enough to pay the higher prices. That is how supply and demand operates in the marketplace of a capitalistic economic system.

The "supply and demand" law applies both to products a company might make, and to an employee and what (s)he might earn based on his or her value in the workplace. The supply of a product or service can be subject to varying demand, as can the supply of people in the workforce with any particular skill. The earlier example of the superior sports athlete applies perfectly here. There are very few superstars in any sport. They are the ones that have the most influence on the success of the teams. Naturally, they are in the highest demand, because their supply is very limited. Their compensation packages therefore exceed those of other players. Things like salary caps may interfere, but the goal of the team management is almost always to pay extra to keep top talent with the home team. The same is true in the corporate world.

At the other extreme, people with no significant job skills are not in short supply. There are many of them, and the demand for them is low. As a result, their value to companies is generally minimal, and they might be lucky to be offered a very low paying job. If they accept a low paying job, it is their decision. Nobody forces it on them. They accept it because it is better for them than the alternative of no income at all, and it is the best job they can find. They are paid minimally because the company doesn't perceive their potential contribution as sufficient to want them enough to offer them more money. Also because there are many other people willing to work for the same low pay and take any job they can get. Historically, those low end jobs were "starter" jobs. McDonald's restaurants used to pride itself on its employee turnover of close to 100%. The company realized that it provided jobs to those who were in the process of getting an education or learning a skill, and helping them pay their bills while they prepared themselves for higher paying jobs.

The government mandates that employers pay employees a minimum wage. Much like the bureaucrats in a socialist country that decide businesses' production levels and wages and prices, many predominantly capitalistic countries have implemented partial wage controls in the form of a minimum wage that basically applies to all industries. The argument is that companies would not pay unskilled workers fairly unless government forced them to pay a certain minimum. But very often, this disrupts the market. When a company can make a profit only by hiring a group of people at less than minimum wage, those jobs will never materialize even if there is an abundant supply of people who would be glad to take them. The company isn't going to engage in operations that have no chance of becoming profitable. Minimum wage laws have been labeled as "entry level job prevention" laws.

As some localities have mandated higher minimum wage laws, we see companies eliminating jobs like taking orders at fast food restaurants or check-out clerks at department stores. Self-order-placing kiosks and self-checkout machines become more cost effective and commonplace when the alternative of a person becomes significantly more expensive, and the demand for the products at higher the prices necessary to pay for the higher labor costs, drops off. (This is due to insufficient price "elasticity.") While some people might get a raise due to revised minimum wage laws, many more will not get an entry level opportunity in the first place. This is a consequence of the government passing laws that conflict with the law of supply and demand for employees. The government might as well pass a law that mandates the force of gravity be reduced for elderly and obese people. At least that law wouldn't prevent people from getting jobs. Like the law of gravity, the law of supply and demand cannot be legislated. People who advocate socialism don't understand that.

Occasionally we see news stories of companies offering multi-million dollar compensation packages to CEO's at other companies, to come over and lead them to better profitability. It happens all the time. That is supply and demand in action. The CEO's don't force anyone to make them offers. Those offers are based on the value a CEO is likely to add to the new company. They are in high enough demand (due to short supply) to justify the expense of a lucrative compensation package. It is also an example of how under capitalism, companies tend to shift assets, including workers, to where they can do the most good. The sports team may shift a player to a different position, or it may trade the player for one from another team, all to improve the team's performance. Under capitalism, businesses do exactly the same thing, for exactly the same reason.

The key functional difference between capitalism and socialism in the workplace, is that capitalism allows and supports financially rewarding superior productivity and results, while socialism generally prohibits financially rewarding superior results. Socialism is predicated on every worker doing his or her best in the first place, so providing financial incentive to achieve more would therefore make no sense. Plus it wouldn't be fair to everybody else. Socialism actually rewards under-performing employees by paying them at the same level as more productive employees, thereby removing any incentive for anyone to work harder. In the real world, this dramatically decreases productivity.

History has shown poor worker productivity to be inevitable whenever socialism is implemented. The main appeal of socialism is its perceived fairness. What is usually overlooked is that it accomplishes that fairness by eventually making almost everybody equally poor. (In our society today, many people consider the "fairness" of equal income more desirable than everyone having much more income opportunity. Usually the people who believe that are the victims of the US education system.) But the most serious downside of true socialism, is that it requires a dictatorship in order to keep it operating indefinitely. History has proven that socialism is very often a short step away from Communism, with the Communist party leadership acting as the dictator. Communism restricts individual freedom and liberties, and it impedes the creation of wealth and an improved quality of life.

CHAPTER 2

WEALTH IS GOOD REGARDLESS OF HOW IT IS DISTRIBUTED

Wealth in a society enables the creation and maintenance of the society's infrastructure, education systems, social programs, national defense, and more. Wealthy people pay disproportionately more taxes than everybody else, whether it be sales taxes, income taxes (unless a "flat tax is adopted), property taxes, capital gains taxes, or other taxes. Wealthy people by necessity spend their money and spread their wealth throughout society. People often get distracted by how the wealth in a society is distributed. In other words, how many people get very big paychecks vs. how many people get much smaller paychecks.

It is common for people who don't know better to decry disparities in income and wealth in a country. They think that the presence of super rich in a population of primarily middle (or lower) class, is a bad thing. Often they have a vague perception that wealthy people somehow got their wealth at the expense of others. Except for personal injury attorneys and politicians, that is very seldom a valid assumption. People don't understand that regardless of the distribution of wealth across the different social strata of a society, more wealth is better for the quality of life of all the citizens of a country. The problem may be a lack of middle class. A surplus of very wealthy people is never a problem. Eliminating wealthy people by any means would hurt, not help, everybody else.

A statistic under the Obama administration showed that the top 10 percent of US income earners paid 71 percent of the federal income tax burden while the lowest earning 47 percent of Americans paid no income taxes at all. Yet many people think those top performing people who pay all those taxes are a bad thing. That is usually due to the erroneous perception that the wealthy somehow managed to acquire their wealth at the expense of the lower paid wage earners. The next chapter will expose the fallacy of that notion. The important thing to understand is that more wealth is better for a society, regardless of how it is distributed. The average person at the poverty level in the United States has a higher standard of living than the average person in the average socialist country. Plus, (s)he has the opportunity to do much better in the future because the capitalistic system allows and encourages upward mobility, unlike socialistic systems. The importance of that cannot be overstated.

When people have more wealth, they generally do either one of two things with it. Either they spend it or they save it, or some combination. Even if they give it away, the recipients then either spend it or save it. When money is spent, it flows through the normal channels of retail purchasing, rent and mortgage payments, utilities, etc.

In a healthy economy, it also flows through "cracks" in the "regular" economy, in ways that benefit many people that do not have traditional jobs. Street vendors selling caricature drawings of passersby or perhaps selling cheese covered bagels, would never be possible if the passersby were all poor. Such micro-businesses are below the radar of normal business managers and city planners. They offer goods and services that require people walking by to have discretionary spending money. Ironically, it is the artists and creative people in a society that are often the most strident proponents of socialism instead of capitalism. Presumably they feel that they would be compensated the same as everyone else under socialism, thereby making more money. That would be half right.

They are ignorant of the lessons of history. Societies that chose socialism (or had it imposed) have far less wealth and therefore far lower disposable income spread across the population. The point though, is that with more wealth per capita under capitalism, more people have more ability to buy sidewalk caricatures, or anything else that an aspiring street vendor might try to sell. One merely has to compare the downtown areas of major cities in wealthy countries, to the downtown areas of relatively poor countries.

And the same concept applies to more common discretionary purchase decisions by consumers. Concert tickets or CDs, movie tickets or DVDs, and books and magazines, provide temporary entertainment. The artists and purveyors of these entertainment media depend on an abundance of people having enough money to buy these things after they cover their expenses for necessary things like rent or mortgage, utilities, food, clothing, taxes, etc. In socialist countries, few people can afford such luxuries. There is no industry comparable to Hollywood, in Russia or Communist China, or any other socialist country. That reduces the opportunities for musicians, actors, artists, and other creative types to work in careers that best fit their abilities and passions. Ditto for waiters in restaurants or sales reps in high end stores, and so many other people. In the old Soviet Union, artists were paid by the government to create art in order to enhance the prestige of the government. But freedom of artistic expression was limited.

One of the benefits of more wealth in a society is that people have far more options to earn a primary or secondary income. And with an affluent society, there is a tremendous number of people who take a chance at starting their own companies. In socialist countries, such opportunities are virtually non-existent. In addition to the shortage of potential customers in those countries, the state determines what businesses can operate, and how much the employees there can make.

When people set aside a portion of their income for savings, it almost always winds up in some type of investment. After all, who doesn't want their money to grow? Examples are stocks (equities), bonds, and certificates of deposit (CDs), or just savings accounts at the local bank. In all of those examples, the money being saved in investments becomes available to loan to others to start or expand businesses. That of course, leads to more job creation. More robust job creation puts pressure on employers to pay their employees more. Once again, it gets back to supply and demand, for the labor market. When sufficient wealth is created for people to have enough left over after paying for their basic needs, savings and investment becomes commonplace. In general, investment leads to new companies and fuels job. In a socialistic country, none of this is possible. The level of overall wealth necessary to drive that process is never available.

Another benefit of wealthy people and an uneven level of wealth in a society is a more effective self-correcting process for economies that have entered an inevitable downward (recession) cycle of economic activity and employment. Since the early to mid-twentieth century, capitalist economic policy has been strongly influenced by the thoughts and writings of an English economist named John Maynard Keynes ("Kanes"). A brief and simplistic explanation of a primary aspect of Keynes' theories is that when capitalist economies are in recession cycles, it is due to a lack of demand for products. That's what happens when people become unemployed and don't have money to buy the quality and quantity of things they once bought.

The Keynes economic model was widely embraced in capitalist countries for many decades, and continues to have its advocates today. Keynes' solution to recessions was for the government to implement deficit spending to get money into the hands of consumers to drive production up and therefore put people back to work making things. But deficit spending comes with the penalty of increasing the national debt, which adds to the tax burden on everyone in the future.

It also skews the natural order of the supply and demand levels of an economy. It creates an artificial demand by offering products that otherwise would not be produced until some point in the future. It tends to "borrow" demand that people have for things in future weeks, months, and years, by causing them to be purchased in the short term. If someone buys a new car every ten years, and government money to stimulate the economy induces them to buy one in the short term instead of waiting five more years as they normally would have, they probably won't buy their next car for ten more years instead of maybe five years as would have normally occurred. That tends to inhibit future economic growth levels to fix the short term problem. There is widespread (but not total) agreement among economists that US President Franklin Roosevelt (FDR) drastically prolonged the Great Depression that started in 1929. He introduced aspects of a command (socialistic) economy, and stifled capitalistic forces in the economy.

An economy with uneven levels of personal wealth and a significant percentage of wealthy people has an advantage in self-correcting its way out of recessions. As a recession progresses, economic activity declines, and the demand for goods and services diminishes. But when it is suppressed, the pressure for new goods and services gradually increases. People's things wear out. Their clothes and cars and furniture wear out. They still have more kids and need new things for them which are a struggle to afford. At this point, the people who have more money than the general population, are the ones who are going to start reacting to the increased pressure to buy new things. Unlike their poorer countrymen, they can still afford to. Their wealth then starts being infused into the economy, and people gradually start returning to work to start providing a bit more goods and services again. Then the process starts to take off, and those people able to work get paychecks and start responding to their own pent up demand for things. As that happens, more and more people go back to work and the economy recovers. The more wealthy people that can drive this process in the first place, the sooner the economy recovers, and the less severe the recession is likely to be.

Clarification of the definition of the common term "supply side" economics is in order. While Keynesian economic theory holds that government spending will spur the economy by increasing the production and supply of goods and services and jobs, it is quite different from the theory and practice to which "supply side" economic theory refers today. "Supply side" refers to a policy of minimal government involvement in the economy, including minimal taxes and regulatory burdens, so businesses have reduced obstacles to their success.

CHAPTER 3

THE SIMPLE LOGIC OF HOW WEALTH IS CREATED

The logic of how wealth is actually created is a very powerful concept to understand. It is not taught in any classes. Almost nobody knew it before this book was published. Here is a simple example using simple logic. Consider the total wealth of the United States, say, in 1850. In other words, the combined value of the assets of every person and business, plus the government. That year, the country was the same geographical size as it is today, excluding Hawaii and Alaska. The population was approximately 23 million people. There were no paved roads, tall buildings, or airports. Electrical power generation did not exist. Indoor plumbing was virtually non-existent. The transcontinental railroad was still 13 years from starting construction. Horses and walking were the primary means of transportation.

Flash forward to 1990, 140 years later. The US population was approximately 250 million people that year. Although the population increased well over tenfold from 1850 to 1990, the average citizen then enjoyed a standard of living that was regarded as among the highest in the world. Cars with automatic transmissions and air conditioning were the norm for American families, as were color TVs, electric refrigerators, and a host of other technologies and conveniences that didn't even exist in the prior century. By 1990 there were hundreds of cities with skyscrapers in what were once undeveloped woods and prairies. Millions of miles of paved roads, tens of thousands of bridges, and hundreds of airports were added. Along the way, America paid for the lead role in both world wars. It then paid for the reconstruction of a devastated post-WWII Europe, and provided similar assistance to Japan.

So ..... where did the staggering sums of money come from to pay for all this? Did the government just print it? The short answer is: no. That would have only created an economy-collapsing inflation debacle. The value of things is usually determined by the amount of resources including labor necessary to create them, not on how much money is printed. Printing more money doesn't reduce the materials and labor necessary to create things. It just dilutes the value of the existing money. The same money just becomes worth less, meaning the economy experiences inflation.

Well then .... did third world populations get pillaged for their buried treasures or secret Swiss bank account contents? While some people seem to think such things, the math doesn't come even remotely close to adding up. You can't get rich by taking money from people who have none. The wealth to create so many shining cities and an enviable standard of living for a dramatically expanded population could only have been created.

The key question then, is HOW was, and is, that wealth created? To understand this simple concept, is to understand what so many people, especially politicians, just don't know.

Simply put, wealth is created by individuals and companies, when they add value. For example, when a company spends $20 million/year on raw materials, and it converts those raw materials (into a more valuable form) to create actual products worth $50 million, the difference is $30 million. Maybe it's a medical devices company that purchased cheap bulk plastic granules which it converts into expensive plastic transfusion pumps. Or maybe it's an automotive supplier that converts rolled sheet metal into elaborate car body parts. Either way, $30MM of new wealth is created, since the newly created products could be readily converted into dollars, simply by exchanging them for currency (selling them), in the marketplace. In these examples, the company has effectively printed (created) its own money by "printing" (creating) its products which it easily exchanges for money. And of course that money becomes salaries for the employees who collectively worked to create it. In a capitalistic system, the money gets distributed to the employees, again, based on the laws of supply and demand. The rare CEO whose moxie can make the company more successful, thus helping it create more wealth and more jobs, generally gets far more compensation than the easily replaced assembler ... much to the consternation of well meaning but ignorant people obsessed with "fairness." And from the employees, the wealth gets pumped into the economy (other companies) as they live their lives and buy everything from toilet paper to homes. In doing so, new businesses, and jobs and profits in other industries, are created. As that happens, more companies are spawned which hire more employees and then add to the overall wealth creation process, otherwise known as "value added".

The process is self-perpetuating. It is organically self-seeding in terms of new companies starting up, and often expands as long as market saturation or inhibiting factors like taxes and regulations do not grow to a point where businesses must struggle to grow or even survive. It is all based on adding value to create new wealth. The prior examples were in the manufacturing arena, where almost all production activity adds value.

But the same value added process often occurs in the service or other non-manufacturing industries. Computer consultants can make enterprise computing systems more efficient, thus making them more valuable. Cab drivers and airline pilots provide transportation services that people sometimes use to conduct business, adding to their value in some cases by putting them where they are most effective. Perhaps thanks to a taxi driver, an airline pilot is a lot more valuable in the cockpit. Farmers turn their land, plus seeds, labor, and maybe fertilizer, into crops that have a higher level of value. Grocery and other retail stores, enable shoppers to conveniently see and touch and buy the products they want, by bringing the products close to the shoppers' location. If shoppers see fresh strawberries that look good, they are more valuable to the shopper than strawberries pictured on a web site that might not be so fresh and won't be instantly available to take home. Not all service industries correlate to wealth creation. Lawn care services provide temporary aesthetic improvements to people's yards, but they usually fall far short of raising the value of the property. Not all services add value. In those cases, money is just exchanged, without any wealth creation.

Some might argue that when companies generate wealth, the money isn't being created, but merely transferred from the buyer to the seller, which would produce no net growth. That is refuted by simple logic. When the economy is good, most companies grow their revenues. Not just some at the expense of others, which would yield zero net growth. There would be no such thing as economic growth if the amount of collective wealth was constant. (Plus, that ignores the question of where the wealth came from in the first place.) Conversely, when the economy is bad, we see a majority of companies struggling to survive, often unsuccessfully.

There are no winners that benefit from the negative balance sheets of the losers. Additionally, employees can't keep getting paid week after week if all the companies are just passing the same money around.

It's undeniable that wealth creation is taking place when companies are allowed to pursue their profit objectives, creating or adding value in the process. But when capitalistic governments enact burdensome legislation that makes it harder and harder for companies to survive and keep people employed, they are shutting down the only things that prevent their countries from becoming third world countries .... their wealth engines ... the companies. Every job a government suppresses through what amounts to anti-business policies, removes money flow into the economy. No paycheck gets pumped into the economy to buy things if it the person gets laid off. And like the classic death spiral, an ever increasing number of people that would have been employed, then become dependent on the government, which does not create wealth. The government routinely takes wealth in the form of taxes by depleting the bank accounts of those who created it, and gives it to those who do nothing to create it.

There is an undeniable moral imperative to support people by allocating wealth where it is truly needed. But often the process becomes corrupted, inefficient, and excessive. Providing benefits to those who are able but chose not to work constitutes excessiveness. When major welfare reform was implemented during the Clinton administration, it not only contributed to reducing the tax burdens on everyone, it often helped welfare recipients more than anyone else. It gave them the push they needed to re-enter the workforce. For some families, it broke a multigenerational cycle of welfare dependency. While taxes for social programs are necessary, taxes and regulations reduce the ability of companies to invest in their own growth. They limit wealth creators in using their wealth to grow and create more jobs. And it often turns people who would otherwise have an opportunity to grow a career and make something of their lives, into those who are stuck in a perpetual cycle of dependency, with little hope for anything more. The destructiveness on every level of business suppressing policies is well documented.

Under both the Reagan and Trump administrations, corporate tax rates were drastically reduced. As a result, the money that didn't go to the government as taxes, allowed companies to invest in new products and markets and to grow. In both instances it led to dramatic growth in the economy and in job creation that hadn't been seen in decades prior to each of those events. Yet politicians and pundits have consistently claimed that each dollar spent on welfare or unemployment insurance payouts, yields a net increase in the GDP (Gross Domestic Product) over and above that dollar. The argument goes that the welfare money stimulates economic growth when the recipients buy necessities. If that were true, then more money to more people on welfare and unemployment recipients would create a stronger economy. Not only does that fly in the face of common sense, but history has consistently demonstrated that having far fewer people on welfare including unemployment payments, is enormously advantageous for the economy. Paying people benefits with money that could otherwise create jobs, to stay home and not help companies create wealth, is only a drain on the economy.

Yet depending on the government leaders in charge at any given time, such business inhibiting policies sometimes expand unabated as if by design. Then they diminish or eliminate companies, wealth, and people's opportunities to participate in the dream of a better life. Those consequences affect people of every demographic category. Ironically, this pending misery is always sold to voters under the banner of fairness.

Socialist countries don't get to have the problems of over taxation or government burdens in the form of regulations. Their industries are so inefficient, that the bureaucrats don't normally view them as lucrative tax revenue sources. To try to minimize social discontent, socialistic governments strive to keep as many people employed as possible. That is the primary goal. Socialist economic policy is itself a terrible regulatory burden. It is due as much to an inefficient business process than regulations, but the net effect is the same. Socialistic governments appear to understand their own handicaps. They tend to try to reduce other burdens to compensate for their own administrative burdens. After the fall of the Iron Curtain (the Berlin Wall), it was revealed that socialist East Germany had been dumping horribly polluting chemicals into convenient (inexpensive) landfills, resulting in serious long term environmental damage.

Sometimes there are industries like oil or coal production that allow the socialistic government to collect profits from international sales, but the production of goods and services is not driven by a profit motive like it is in capitalistic economies. That results in many useless goods and services being offered. None of the people doing the work benefit from the company doing better. To the contrary, they benefit by being protected if the company fails. So the company plods along if it is constantly pushed, but profits and growth are minimal at best. And when all the companies in the country operate at such a depressed level, that country is absolutely guaranteed to have a low standard of living, barring something unusual like major energy reserves.

CHAPTER 4

WHY WEALTHY PEOPLE ARE BENEFICIAL TO EVERYBODY

It is a popular misconception that it is bad for a few people to have a great deal more wealth than everybody else. Such thinking is based on people's natural inclination to believe that "fairness" is always good. Fairness is a hypothetical construct and it is highly subjective. Is it always fair for two people doing the same job to get the same pay? What if one works twice as hard? Or what if one works half as hard but is three times as productive?

Is it better for all ten people in a group to get paid $100 a day under Plan 1, or is it better to have four people get paid $300/day while four others get $500/day, and the last two get $600/day under Plan 2? Under Plan 2, the lowest paid four people ($300) get only half of what the highest paid people ($600) get. They also make three times what they made under the "fair" Plan 1. So which plan is better? If the priority is fairness, Plan 1 is better. If the priority is everyone being better off, Plan 2 is better. The normal counter-argument is that you could take all the money in Plan 2 and split it up evenly so everyone then gets $440/day. The situation is more complex if the people making $600/day could join a different group and still make at least $600/day. But perhaps if they did that, their old group without them could not even make enough for everyone remaining to get $100/day. This example actually demonstrates the choice between socialism (Plan 1) and capitalism (Plan 2). Is "fair" income equality better than more-but-different income for everyone?

Sometimes people's perceptions of fairness are based on the circumstances. Sometimes they are based on things like people's race or economic status, which have nothing to do with their work ethic or their results. Is it better to award a desirable job to someone who has struggled, vs. someone who had it easy? People in the media routinely decry the income or wealth gap between the wealthiest in society and the average citizens as being excessive. Inherent in their disapproval is the flawed notion that the wealth of the rich would somehow be spread around among the average folks if things were only fairer. Such thinking misunderstands a universal cause and effect relationship. If someone's wealth was attributable to hard work and risk taking and building an organization that created tremendous wealth, is it fair to take it from him and give it to somebody who dropped out of high school and plays video games in his spare time?

The IRS reported that in 2011, the top one percent of the workforce in the US earned 19 percent of the total income, and paid 35 percent of the total tax burden. So they are already paying a disproportionately high percentage of the income taxes. In the same time frame, the bottom fifty percent of wage earners, collectively paid just three percent of the tax burden. Another perspective revealed that if the wealth of all the "wealthy" people was confiscated, it would only be sufficient to fund the federal government for a few months. Then the money would be gone, and the stream of annual tax receipts as well as new business ventures that sprang from those people would come to an abrupt halt.

Thanks to capitalism, the vast majority of people who are "wealthy," have acquired their wealth on their own, versus inheriting it. Either way, they did not acquire it by making anyone else less wealthy. They usually acquired it as a result of some value added process. Acquisition of wealth almost always results from offering customers something those customers wanted. And for those who inherited significant wealth, it was typically acquired initially by a parent or other close family member. Seldom does great wealth get passed down repeatedly through successive generations. The greater wealth of some people does not come from everyone else becoming poorer.

In fact, the opposite is generally true. Not only does having very wealthy people in a society not cost others anything, those others actually benefit indirectly from those with great wealth. It is wealthy people that are far more likely to start a new business and create new job opportunities in the process. It is often wealthy people that spend more patronizing businesses, thus helping them succeed. It is wealthy people who pay disproportionately more taxes than their less affluent neighbors, thus lowering the tax burden on low and middle class workers. The various levels of government can offer more and better services such as new roads or better medical care for the indigent, as a result of the additional tax revenues made possible by the wealthy. Those services disproportionately benefit middle and lower class people.

Understanding that wealth is created by entrepreneurs and companies and employees is important. Many people look at wealth as something that rich people acquire less than honorably then hoard at the expense of poor people. That explains how politicians can use the issue of "fairness" to get people to vote for things like higher taxes on the rich. Very few rich people are given their wealth. Instead they are usually rewarded with wealth by their employers or by the market, for helping to create more of it, which ultimately benefits everyone regardless of income.

Some people have a negative perspective on businesses that operate on a for-profit basis, or don't provide some obvious social benefit. People who work for "non-profit" organizations, frequently exude a personal pride based on a perception that their work is somehow more noble than supporting a company in the pursuit of profit. They have been conditioned to believe, even if only subliminally, that businesses that make a profit, somehow do so at the expense of their customers. They see a one-way transfer of money from the customer to the company as enriching the company at the expense of the customer. They usually miss that the customer would not fork over his or her hard earned money, unless the company was offering them something that they felt was more important to have than the money they were paying. In other words, the customer gets something of value to them, in exchange for their money. And as was just explained, that value typically results from the company's operations creating or adding value.

With this level of understanding of what a business does, some people will think it's acceptable for the business to operate and keep people employed as long as it doesn't profit beyond the ability to pay its bills. Otherwise they think the customer would be exploited. First of all, if the customer feels they are being exploited, they don't have to purchase from the company. Again, potential customers only buy what they want and only if they feel they benefit from the purchase, even knowing the company will make a profit. Many people realize the company needs to make a profit if it is going to stay viable in the long term. But some people don't realize that businesses use their profits to grow the company, improve quality, pay back investors, and other reasons ultimately tied to the success of the business. Companies often use a share of their profits to provide benefits and perks to employees. Profitable larger companies especially, provide employee benefits such as child care services, profit sharing, substance abuse counseling and treatment, annual bonuses, continuing education tuition, etc. Such benefits help companies attract high quality employees, to better compete in the competitive realm of capitalism.

Non-profit organizations often rely on donations to subsidize their operations. And while their operations are often of critical benefit to people, animals, or things (such as historic buildings, or polluted areas), they don't compare to for-profit businesses in creating the wealth that benefits society as a whole. Far more often than not, the donations that the non-profits rely on to survive and help others, come directly or indirectly from wealth generated by for-profit businesses. Business enterprises that create wealth are a benefit everyone, including the disadvantaged. They can benefit everyone even if they don't engage in any socially appealing practices that specifically help the disadvantaged. Non-profits generally provide a focused benefit to only those that they specifically target to help. Although working for a non-profit organization is usually considered noble, working for a for-profit enterprise should usually be considered at least as noble. Financial generosity would not be possible without the wealth created by for-profit companies.

CHAPTER 5

SEE JACK CREATE NEW WEALTH

Let's assume Jack is working at a machine shop. One day Jack decides to start his own machine shop. After several years of scrimping and saving and planning, he gives up the security of a steady paycheck and takes out a second mortgage on his home to buy the machines and other equipment he needs, and to rent the space for his new business. He works long hours, sacrificing time with his family. He assumes the roles of salesperson, bookkeeper, designer, machine maintenance technician, jig and fixture maker, machinist, and janitor.

Chances are, Jack's business will fail within the first couple years. Seventy percent of businesses with employees fail in less than ten years. Overall, the number is over 96 percent and 80% fail in under 18 months. But let's assume for the sake of example, that Jack becomes successful on his first attempt. Perhaps he comes up with a slick way of modifying the gear hubs that his biggest customer buys from him, which allows him to make the part with a special ridge that causes lubrication to stay in the hub area longer when the part is used by his customers. That improves its reliability, and helps his customers cut downtime and maintenance and lubricant costs. Soon Jack's business is expanding and he's hiring people for two shifts. He is able to pay them a competitive wage, and offer them health and retirement benefits. Out of nothing, Jack created a company that produced goods and services, adding value in the process.

Continuing with this example, let's say Jack's company generated $5 million in sales a year. The actual numbers are not important except as examples, but let's further assume that his cost for materials, and energy and other overhead to run his business was only $500,000 ($½ million) per year. Then, he paid his employees two million in salaries, and spent another two million on their "burden" including their benefits, vacation pay, social security payments, and other government taxes. Over the course of the year, he was able to pay himself the remaining $500,000.

In one year, Jack spent $500,000 on the things he needed to make his products, and sold those products for $5 million. He and his employees therefore created $4,500,000 in new wealth that year. That wealth paid his employees' salaries, and enabled them to live and raise families. It paid taxes to the government. It enabled Jack to build a big house and put lots of money in the bank.

The money Jack spent on his house helped employ carpenters, bricklayers, plumbers, electricians, roofers, landscapers, and more. Because his house was expensive, he paid three times as much property taxes as his neighbors. Jack's house was expensive because the construction workers added value to the raw materials like bricks and lumber converting it into a nice big house. His tax district (and the people living in it) benefited more from Jack than anyone else in his neighborhood. The money he put in the bank became available for the bank to loan to other people seeking to borrow money for homes or businesses of their own.

The salaries that Jack's employees received enabled them to buy cars and homes and furniture and children's clothes. That helped the car companies and the clothing companies and restaurants they patronized create more wealth. Just like Jack's company converted $500,000 of raw products into $5 million in new products, the car companies and diaper companies and the restaurants did much the same thing with their portion of the wealth created by Jack's and other peoples' companies. They used the money to buy materials and pay their employees and make their products to create new wealth too.

Jack's customers who bought his gear hubs created even more wealth because of Jack. Because of Jack's unique ridged design, they can spend less while producing at least the same amount of products as before. When companies reduce the cost of their products to their customers, those customers have more money to spend on other goods and services, or to put into savings. It's sort of like companies that make things giving their customers a slight raise in income, because those customers don't have to spend as much to get what they want or need. At the end of the day, the net result is the same. They have more money in their pockets after they buy something, compared to the last time they bought the item, as if they had gotten a bit of a pay raise. In this way, people's standard of living is increased, even when they don't make any more money.

Every year, Jack and his business create millions of dollars in wealth. Every year, that wealth passes through the economy and some of it creates additional wealth for others. The wealth of those others was used to create still more wealth, and on and on, like a chain reaction running out of control.

The process of wealth creation is normally facilitated through banking transactions. Companies and people send money between their accounts and the accounts of those with whom they are doing business, in order to collect payments and to make payments. Money is seldom handled as currency except by consumers. As the amount of money in banks increases due to wealth creation, governments add money to their money supplies, to maintain a certain "liquidity ratio" of the money available to be withdrawn as cash, to the total amount in everyone's accounts. When the amount of money in the bank accounts of people and businesses increases because of wealth creation, governments use different means to increase the money supply proportionately. They can back it up by printing cash in controlled amounts greater than the amount printed to replace worn out bills.

Jack is but one example of how wealth is created in America's capitalistic economy. The inevitable conclusion is that companies that add value as they operate are the source of the wealth of a society. So for a society to do well economically, companies must be allowed to operate and become successful. Punishing companies by taxing or regulating them excessively, will stifle wealth creation, and reduce most people's standard of living. It is easy to see why throughout history and to this day, capitalist countries have consistently and dramatically outperformed socialist countries economically, and their citizens have enjoyed a higher standard of living. Companies in capitalistic economic systems have a huge advantage in creating wealth.

There are no corresponding examples of how this wealth creation example would work in a socialist economy. That is because it wouldn't. Recall the first paragraph of this chapter in which Jack takes great risk and makes great sacrifices to start his own business. Obviously he did these things with the goal of becoming financially successful at some point. While he may have had other motives, like being the boss, or leaving a company for his children to inherit, they would not be compelling enough for him to risk losing his house and putting his household deeply in debt. In a socialist economy, the potential for an uncommonly high income and level of wealth as well as ownership of a business enterprise does not exist. So all those people Jack's company hired would never have gotten those jobs. They would have never passed their incomes from the wealth they created at Jack's company into the economy for other businesses to grow and in turn create more wealth. Jack could not have any hope of transforming his life for the better, and transitioning from a marginally paid factory worker to a successful business owner. Only in a capitalist economy, can you see the Jacks of society create new wealth, and the new jobs and a wealthier society which results from their risk taking and their successes.

CHAPTER 6

VALUE ADDED THROUGH REAL ESTATE APPRECIATION

What this means is that the value of things can increase over time, or appreciate, with no other work required. In lieu of the sale of goods or services with added value, an alternative avenue of wealth creation is by the use of investment tools. Many older people saw their net worth increase significantly over their lifetime as a result of appreciation in the value of their homes. This is a secondary effect of wealth creation through value added. Real estate values rise as a result of rising demand. The rise in demand for real estate results from the rising size and affluence of a population. That is attributable to wealth creation by the businesses that employ the people who are helping to add value, since that newly created wealth is paid to those people as salaries. Home prices can only go up as fast or as far as the availability of a market of buyers who have enough money to afford more expensive homes. If there are only ten wealthy people shopping in a market where a thousand people are trying to sell high end homes, the sellers are going to have to slash their sale prices to have any chance of getting any money at all for their homes.

This exaggerated scenario is another example of "supply and demand." In this example, the abundant supply of very expensive homes is very high relative to the demand, based on the presence of only ten potential buyers. So the prices decline to meet the low demand. The example represents what is called a "buyer's market."

In a capitalistic market, investment appreciation takes place in a myriad of ways. But the reason they work is because the laws of supply and demand are working in the background, in whatever markets the investment is made.

In a socialistic market, private property such as housing is often either discouraged or forbidden by the government, or there is no availability of extra wealth to trigger the construction of new housing, even if government bureaucrats were to decree it. New construction is decreed then funded by the government. So wealth creation by investment in real estate is generally not an option in socialist countries. When the demand for things is stifled because people have barely enough money to survive, few expensive things are in demand so they don't increase in value. And if the value of the housing did increase, it wouldn't benefit the residents because the government owns it.

CHAPTER 7

ENFORCING SOCIALISM

In the preceding chapter, the presence of more wealthy people meant more potential buyers, more demand, and the likelihood of higher sale prices for the real estate. In a capitalistic system, this is all natural and good. In a socialistic system, the problem is the existence of high end homes in the first place. Socialists come into power based on the promise that everybody will become economically equal, which for the poorer people in the population holds great appeal. Socialists believe people should not aspire to own such homes or ever acquire sufficient wealth to own them. For to do so, would not be fair to those who owned less. The goal is to have income and wealth parity.

It is detrimental to a society to have too few or no wealthy people. As explained in Chapter 4, more wealthy people rather than fewer is invariably better for everyone. But that thinking does not apply in the context of a "socialist utopia." How many times have you heard someone on TV mentioning the big wealth gap between the very rich and everybody else, as if it was detrimental to everybody else? A great deal of socialistic thinking permeates the American mainstream media. If someone becomes more and more wealthy by creating more and more wealth for the economy and good jobs for others, does it not make sense to celebrate his or her success and hope for more people like that? Not to a socialist.

So what is the "solution" to having some very wealthy people in a society? That question reflects the flawed thinking of socialists that wealth inequality is bad and therefore needs a "solution." The primary way to achieve income and wealth parity is to make sure everyone gets the same share of the economic pie through wage and price controls. Under a socialist economic system, the CEO and the mail room clerk get the same share of the pie, when they get comparable paychecks. In reality, there is no CEO under socialism. Despite the foolishness of this policy, government bureaucrats make the leadership decisions for the companies, negating the need for CEOs. The point remains that every worker in the company and in the overall economy, gets the same basic share of the economic pie, regardless of their contribution level. As has been explained, a socialistic economy does an abysmal job of creating wealth. So the amount of wealth available to be distributed evenly throughout the overall society is insufficient for the people to have a standard of living that is in any way comparable to one in an otherwise comparable capitalistic country.

People who advocate socialism for the US, look at all the wealth being produced, and see it being distributed unfairly. Even if one accepts their premise that it's good to take money from those who earned it and give it to those who didn't, one can't ignore the fact that wealth creation would quickly drop to relatively low levels, and there would be little to redistribute.

In a socialist utopia, people would struggle and sacrifice as if they could be rewarded with great wealth, but understand and accept that no such increased wealth was allowed to them as individuals. They would do it for the good of the collective. It should be clear to the reader that this scenario is inconsistent with human nature. Few people consistently sacrifice for no personal or family benefit. One of the characteristics of work in the factories in the Eastern Bloc (Soviet controlled Eastern European) socialist countries was that there were a number of supervisors whose sole job it was to make sure everybody else was working as hard as they should. Sometimes the number of those supervisors approached the number of actual workers. In the socialistic economy, there is no benefit to hard work, so people are constantly monitored and pushed. The socialist doctrine of fairness means you will make the same whether your productivity is in the top one percent of workers, or the bottom one percent. Why would anyone stress themselves to be in the top one percent, or even the top 50 percent? There is no answer to that question. There is minimal if any incentive to be productive in a socialist workforce, which explains the horrible productivity and insignificant value added (wealth created) by industries in socialistic economies.

Besides wage and price controls, how else does the government impose income equality when some people would find a way to become wealthy while others would do as little as possible? The government either forbids the attempt to start a new business, or simply takes (by taxing) the entrepreneur's wealth away from them after they acquire it.

Capitalists would argue that the second option is morally wrong. It is also problematic for the society because anyone who anticipates more of his or her profits being confiscated is naturally far less likely to incur debt or risk his savings to invest in creating more profits in the first place. What would be the point? So the organic infusion of private sector capital to stimulate the creation of wealth never happens. Everything a socialistic government does to impose fairness, works to the detriment of everyone.

During the transition from capitalism to socialism, the government, as the taxing entity, receives a windfall from taxing a big chunk of profit away from business owners to reduce their incomes so that they are on a par with everyone else. But as time goes on, and there are fewer and fewer such owners and businesses to tax, the government loses a major component of its tax revenues. This is especially true when the government "nationalizes" (takes) peoples' businesses. Metaphorically speaking, the government has then killed its flock of golden geese that were laying those golden eggs. How governments always respond to declining tax revenues from one group, is raise taxes on other groups. Understanding this makes it apparent again that everyone else benefits indirectly from profitable entrepreneurs and companies by not having their taxes raised, or raised as much. And everyone still receives benefits like infrastructure improvements and other things upon which tax revenues are spent. So taking away the incentive for businesses and entrepreneurs to make lots of profit is destructive to any economy. It works to the detriment of everyone in that economy, regardless of income.

Lastly, the imposition of "fairness" can be inflicted by the imposition of regulatory "reforms." The definition of "reform" is: "the improvement or amendment of what is wrong, corrupt, unsatisfactory, etc." What is wrong or unsatisfactory to one person, may be, and often is, quite ideal to another. When these reforms are imposed by the government, it is often to fix what is "wrong" in the eyes of politicians. As you might expect, if those wrongs are all based on some people making more money than others, the people that are making more are not going to perceive something to punish their success as a "reform." What politicians call reforms, business owners often call "burdens" and "obstacles." When government forces even unprofitable companies to provide expanded and costly benefits to employees, the politicians pat themselves on the back and run for re-election based on watching out for the little guy. Then they wonder why companies move their operations offshore or go out of business and all those little guys are out of work.

The ironic consequence of enforced "fairness" is inevitably a decrease in wealth generation, which hurts everyone, directly or indirectly. This is why socialist countries are horrible at wealth generation, especially compared to capitalist countries. It was covered in chapter 2, that more wealth is better. So less wealth is worse. And much less wealth is much worse. There are no examples in the history of civilization, where socialism was superior to capitalism, all other things being equal. When countries convert from capitalism to socialism, life gets worse for all of the citizens. When they go the other way, life gets better. It never fails.

CHAPTER 8

SOCIALISM IN THE MODERN WORLD

Prior to 1991, the former Soviet Union was an alliance of a dozen states under communist rule centered in Moscow, the capital of Russia. Moscow also controlled 11 other "Eastern Bloc" countries. All of these countries were forced to maintain socialistic economies, under threat of military force. The threat was real. In 1956, Russia invaded Hungary after that country attempted to withdraw from Russia's control. Thousands of Hungarians died when the Russia crushed Hungary's attempt at freedom and democracy and capitalism. In 1968, the Russian military did the same thing for the same reason in Czechoslovakia.

The standard of living in the Eastern Bloc countries was dramatically lower than in the adjacent Western European countries. The difference was due simply to the fact that the Eastern Bloc countries, along with the Soviet Union, utilized a socialistic economic system. Conversely, the Western European nations operated under capitalism. Germany is a good case study because prior to the end of WWII, it had not been split into East

Germany (socialist) and West Germany (capitalist). After the war, it became two separate countries as a result of Germany's defeat by both the US and its allies, and the Soviet Union. Germany remained two separate countries with different economic systems until 1991, when reunification took place. Since recovering from the devastation of WWII, West Germany thrived economically under capitalism, and its citizens prospered. Conversely, East Germany languished economically under socialism, and its citizens endured relatively poor living conditions, and a lack of freedom. In 1961, the Berlin Wall was built to stem the exodus of East Germans seeking a better life in West Germany. Most East Germans who tried to escape across the wall were shot yet many still made the attempt.

It's easy to contrast East and West Germany, because they were one country that split into two economic systems, with the resulting difference being dramatic. Germany was a microcosm of Europe. The same economic system differences existed between the Western European and Eastern European countries. The socialistic Eastern Bloc countries controlled by Moscow suffered economically compared to the countries of Western Europe. The people of Eastern Europe also lived under the oppression of Communism. Their rights as citizens were severely curtailed compared to level of individual freedoms available to Western European and other capitalistic country's citizens. Those Western European countries created much more wealth than their Eastern European neighbors. It was distributed throughout the population in a way that continuously rewarded and incentivized further wealth creation, and provided an elevated standard of living for whole populations. The contrast was stark.

Today, we see the same contrast between socialism and capitalism in Korea. North Korea, operating under a Communist government and a socialistic economic system, cannot even reliably feed its own population. In sharp contrast, the capitalistic economic system of South Korea has lifted the South Korean population out of the poverty that followed the Korean War. It provided the South Korean people with one of the highest standards of living in the world.

The country of Venezuela, is a good "before and after" example of capitalism versus socialism. It went from being one of the most prosperous countries in the Western Hemisphere, to one of rampant poverty and oppression, after switching from capitalism to socialism. As with most socialist/Communist countries, a great number of people sought to escape the consequences of socialism, by fleeing the country.

Even with major energy reserves, the Venezuelan economy completely crashed after the government imposed transition to socialism. Under socialism, private businesses were confiscated with no compensation to the owners, and people were expected to work for subsistence wages, regardless of how much they contributed. Naturally, the most important (and well paid, under capitalism) people soon left. The result for the citizens was catastrophic, including hyperinflation, widespread power outages, food riots, starvation, and millions fleeing the country. Political protesters and people seeking the basic necessities for life were routinely murdered, following a national campaign to confiscate civilian guns. This is the most current example of a country transitioning from capitalism to socialism.

If you are reading this and the school you are attending is teaching you that everything is generally okay in Venezuela circa 2019, then you cannot trust your school to teach the truth. Your school's administration is not alone in demonstrating a willingness to lie to you. Do not think it is an honest mistake. (You should also disbelieve any media outlets that trivialize the problems for the citizens of Venezuela, or abstain from reporting on the exodus of millions of Venezuelans fleeing their beloved country.) If you want to get an accurate assessment of the relative merits of capitalism and socialism, seek out and talk with someone who immigrated to the US or another capitalistic country after living in a socialistic country. Do not waste your time asking a college professor in economics, or sociology, or any other branch of academia. It goes without saying that most politicians are equally worthless sources for accurate information on the subject. Those people will be eager to tell you the beliefs they have chosen to adopt, in order to support their perceptions of what is "right." And they are very convincing, often citing books and experts and cherry picked statistics. But they will be very unlikely to offer information that is accurate. Go instead to someone who is an actual source of firsthand. Anyone born before the early 1960's, that came to the US from Eastern Europe, will likely have that experience and real knowledge of living life under modern socialism. Certainly someone who escaped Venezuela since the imposition of socialism there can also provide firsthand information. Only from such people can you be reasonably assured of learning the real truth.

CHAPTER 9

THE INCLUSIVENESS OF CAPITALISM

Some people say that money is the root of all evil. But the opposite is usually true. While the money that comes from wealth creation enables people to enjoy a higher standard of living regardless of how much they earn, an important positive aspect of capitalism manifests itself in the composition of the workforce. Unlike in socialist societies, companies in a capitalist society exist in a cauldron of competition. Once again, the sports team analogy is very relevant. It should be obvious that sports teams are colorblind when it comes to whom they hire. What matters far more than anything else, is job performance. It is in the best interest of the corporate "team" to have the best people working in their organization. Unlike in the world of professional sports, in the corporate world, there is no need for partitioning men and women due to normal physical differences between the genders. So in the corporate world, race and gender are completely irrelevant compared to a person's ability to positively contribute to the success of the organization.

What person in their right mind would hire a marginal employee of their own race and gender, when they had the option of hiring someone else who could clearly excel at helping them meet their company's or department's business targets? If you were the manager that passed over top talent to hire a lackluster candidate based on race or gender bias, it would have a negative impact both on your department's performance, and your job performance evaluations as a manager. Business people know that managers are graded primarily on the performance of their departments. Departments or companies have a reduced ability to compete in the marketplace when they don't hire the best candidates, regardless of their demographic groups. Biased hiring practices do still exist, but the nature of capitalism is that it ultimately punishes those decisions and people that perpetuate them. While this is obviously true in theory, any objective person with an established career in business will affirm it is very much the norm in the real world workplace as well.

Ironically, it is well meaning politicians who often contribute to minority profiling and discriminatory hiring practices by employers. By passing laws that penalize companies that reassign or replace poor performers if they happen to have a minority status, they cause companies to shy away from hiring minorities in the first place. In today's society, the bigger problem is not employers who discriminate. It is mainly minority candidates who received substandard educations from the US education system. In inner city schools, far more minority children drop out before finishing high school, or graduate despite being functional illiterates, than graduate prepared to go to college.

Social policies to promote equal opportunity are necessary for a healthy and just society. But going about it by punishing wealth creators is not beneficial to anyone. It's especially ironic that the politicians who portray themselves as advocates for the poor and often try to blame discriminatory hiring and promotion practices of businesses for social inequities, are the ones that bear responsibility for the problem of substandard educational opportunities for students in poor inner city neighborhoods. Businesses under capitalism offer the best chance for everyone to lead a better life. And they offer the best chance for minorities to overcome the obstacles to their success that have been created by the government. Businesses value performance above all else. Differences including race, gender, and sexual orientation make no difference because those differences don't affect the bottom line. Not unlike sports teams, businesses put people from different backgrounds in an environment where they work with and support each other. When that happens, everybody comes to learn that attitude and ability are what separate people, not color, gender, etc. Capitalistic businesses offer a surprisingly effective way to battle to the problem of discrimination in a society.

The End

Economics in an Hour

Copyright © 2019
All rights reserved
ISBN 9781092521222

www.ingramcontent.com/pod-product-compliance
Lightning Source LLC
Chambersburg PA
CBHW051204170526
45158CB00005B/1813